SYDNEY WIDE
Spectacular Panoramic Views

PANOGRAPHS®
PUBLISHING PTY LTD

Dominated by its famous Harbour Bridge and Opera House, Sydney is without doubt one of the world's most beautiful cities. Golden beaches, sapphire seas, rivers that flow down from The Blue Mountains into sparkling bays – all create a crown of natural beauty for the magnificent jewel of the city.

The great expanses of water that surround and run through Australia's major gateway provide a wonderful image of freedom in the midst of its activity. The harbour waters, glistening in the sunlight like diamonds, reflect the city's sparkling life. Brisk and dynamic, Sydney is also rich in history, and brimming with a vibrant cosmopolitan culture.

Blessed with a temperate climate, Sydneysiders love outdoor entertainment. On an idyllic Sydney day, the aromas of feasts being cooked on backyard barbeques waft through many pockets of the city.

Like a symphony of life, Sydney's many parts all resonate with their own beauty, yet combine harmoniously in this sensational city of sun and fun.

TITLE PAGE
Sydney Opera House at daybreak

RIGHT
Bondi Beach

Ken Duncan (OAM) was born in Mildura, Victoria, in 1954. A professional photographer since 1980, his work has received many industry awards both in Australia and overseas, and he is now recognized as one of the world's leading panoramic landscape specialists.

Typically casual about such accolades, Ken prefers to say he is just an average photographer with a mighty God. He believes that even in cities we can see the beauty of God's creation all around us. His goal and passion in life is to encourage people to look beyond themselves to something far greater as he tries to capture on film many magical moments in time.

Enjoy the journey as you wander with Ken through the pages of this book, experiencing the wonder of an amazing city.

RIGHT
Spendour of creation

OVERLEAF
Eastern Suburbs aerial

RIGHT
Archibald Fountain, Hyde Park

The Blue Mountains, lying just to Sydney's west, offer magnificent natural scenery and countless opportunities for adventure. Pictured here are the iconic Three Sisters, rising against the deep blue backdrop of the Jamison Valley. These gnarled formations take their name from an Aboriginal story, which relates how a tribal leader turned his three daughters to stone during a battle to protect them from their enemies, only to be killed before he could return them to life. Such stories can add wonderful meaning to our experience of a place. Yet the greatest joy often comes from the moment itself. From heights such as these, we can breathe the fresh mountain air and let our gaze soar over the vast open spaces. The colours of the stone glow in the light, and the sense of peace is profound.

LEFT
Blue Mountain vista

RIGHT
Queen Victoria Building, south end

LEFT
Queen Victoria Building, north end

OVERLEAF
Bronte Beach

Sydney celebration

I love grand old churches. There is a presence about them – the result of all the prayers and praise. St Mary's is Sydney's Catholic cathedral; St Philip's in York Street dates from 1802, and is one of Australia's oldest Anglican churches. In St Mary's I spent many hours waiting and photographing, and saw people from all walks of life visiting the Cathedral. Some came to marvel at the

architecture, but most came seeking help or guidance. I was really touched by one young lady who was obviously very troubled. She wept silently, crying out from a hurting heart. But when she left, it seemed she had found peace and renewed faith. I had a distinct sense that God had heard her prayers and had assigned angels to watch over her.

*Sydney Harbour Bridge from
Jeffrey Street Wharf*

ABOVE
Palm Beach and Barrenjoey headland

ABOVE
Surfer girl, Palm Beach

In the heart of the city, two of Sydney's great stone landmarks provide a link with its colonial past. Both buildings date from the closing decades of the nineteenth century. On the left is the Sydney Town Hall (with its famous clock tower) which was constructed from local "yellow block" sandstone; its design was inspired by various French chateaux and Paris's Hotel de Ville, and it is still sometimes affectionately likened to a wedding cake! On the right, taking up an entire city block, is the lavish, multi-domed Queen Victoria Building completed in 1898. In recent decades this building has been lovingly restored, and it now houses a large array of stylish shops. There are dozens of other historic stone buildings scattered throughout Sydney's Central Business District. They are a constant reminder to the new generation of Sydney's proud heritage.

PREVIOUS PAGES
Pastel sunrise, Freshwater Beach

LEFT
Sydney Town Hall and Queen Victoria Building

For many people, Sydney's connection with the sea helps keep the city sane; when they look out upon the ocean, they enjoy a view untouched by the bustle of urban development. Pictured is a man fishing on Manly Beach, with a gentle mirror-like surf washing towards him over the sand. The sun has newly risen and the air is clean and fresh. It's a beautiful way to start the day! Manly is often seen as the gateway to the Northern Beaches, which stretch from this point as far north as Palm Beach. There is the opportunity to really relax here – to immerse yourself in the beauty of the ocean.

LEFT
Sunrise, Manly Beach

OVERLEAF
Sydney Harbour Bridge Climb

The Australian Reptile Park, one hour north of the city, is one of the best locations for Sydneysiders and visitors to view Australian animals. Here, four koalas sit lazily among the branches, easily fulfilling their role as the nation's cutest ambassadors.

PREVIOUS PAGES
Bondi Beach aerial

RIGHT
Koalas, Australian Reptile Park, Somersby

Elvis the crocodile is one of the Reptile Park's most famous residents. As a Saltwater Crocodile (*Crocodylus porosus*), he shares the dubious distinction of being among Australia's most dangerous predators! But here he is treated with equal amounts of caution and affection.

LEFT
Crocodile, Australian Reptile Park, Somersby

OVERLEAF
Sydney Opera House before dawn

Photography often involves a lot of waiting. On the day of this photograph, the swell was huge and I soon observed that the largest and most dangerous waves were coming in sets about ten minutes apart. Between these mammoth sets, a few potential swimmers approached the chain-fenced ocean pool. I warned them of the lurking danger. After watching for a while they thanked me and wisely turned back. One couple, however, ignored my warning and continued on into the pool. Then, out on the horizon, a gigantic wall of water loomed. When these monster waves hit, the people were thrust into a wall of the pool then sucked towards the open sea. The violent ocean threatened to smash them on the rocks, and they only just managed to grab hold of a safety chain. Battered and bruised, they climbed from the pool and humbly retreated, giving me a nod as they limped on by. It was a salutary reminder of what many Sydneysiders are already aware of: the sea can be dangerous as well as magnificent.

LEFT
Mahon Pool, Maroubra

As I waited in the dark for this shot, there wasn't a single star twinkling through the pre-dawn sky. Usually that means there won't be a great sunrise. In fact it seemed hopeless with the thick overhanging cloud, but I decided to wait and see what the daylight would bring. This photograph just goes to prove that waiting can bring great treasures. As the sun rose, the light was spilled through a great rent along the horizon. It was like a parable: Even in the midst of gloomy and turbulent times, light can break through and transform our circumstances into a spectacle of glory. Hope gives us strength to wait, even when things seem out of control.

RIGHT
Hope and glory, Mona Vale

OVERLEAF
Manly aerial

PREVIOUS PAGES
George Street, The Rocks

ABOVE
Sun seekers, Bronte Beach

ABOVE
Avalon Beach

LEFT
Sunrise reflections, Bayview

OVERLEAF
Coogee sea pool

ABOVE
Old Pyrmont Bridge, Darling Harbour

ABOVE
Bennelong Point, Sydney Harbour

RIGHT
Shark Beach, Nielsen Park

OVERLEAF
Parramatta River, Hunters Hill

The majestic Anzac Bridge spans the waters of Johnstons Bay at Glebe. "Anzac", as a word, was coined during the First World War – an acronym for the Australian and New Zealand Army Corps. Formed in December 1914, the Corps saw its first action on the Gallipoli Peninsula, Turkey, on April 25th, 1915. Over 10,000 Anzacs lost their lives in that campaign alone – one in every four soldiers who landed was killed. As bloody as the battle was, those who survived were then sent to the Western Front where the fighting was even worse. What an enormous price has been paid for our freedom! What do we do with this precious liberty for which so much blood was spilled? Do we take it for granted, or do we stand united for the future of our nation? There can never be too much recognition for those heroes who fought and died. Hopefully this bridge, named in their honour, will be a constant reminder: Lest We Forget.

RIGHT
Sunset, Anzac Bridge

OVERLEAF
Darling Harbour

ABOVE
Fort Denison, Sydney Harbour

ABOVE
Fort Denison, Sydney Harbour

This island off Mrs Macquaries Point was once known as "Pinchgut" because of the deprivations of the convicts there. The tower – built later to defend against a feared Russian attack in the mid nineteenth century – was constructed from 8000 tonnes of sandstone.

The name Bare Island originates from Captain Cook's 1770 observation of "a small, bare island". These days, visitors can cross the wooden bridge for a tour of the old concrete fort – built in the late 1880s to protect Botany Bay from possible sea invasion.

RIGHT
Barrenjoey Head